MY COVID TIME

GLASS

&

RHYME

Verses and Cocktails

Written and Mixed by

GEORGE FORSYTH

*Caroline &
Andy.
For all the
best times,
past,
present
&
future.*

W. H. love,

MAPLE
PUBLISHERS

My Covid Time in Glass & Rhyme

Author: George Forsyth

Copyright © George Forsyth (2021)

The right of George Forsyth to be identified as author of this work has been asserted by the author in accordance with section 77 and 78 of the Copyright, Designs and Patents Act 1988.

First Published in 2021

ISBN: 978-1-914366-81-9 (Paperback)
   978-1-914366-38-3 (Ebook)

Book cover design and Book layout by:
   White Magic Studios
   www.whitemagicstudios.co.uk

Published by:
   Maple Publishers
   1 Brunel Way,
   Slough,
   SL1 1FQ, UK
   www.maplepublishers.com

I dedicate this book to every key worker who worked, tirelessly, to keep us safe and well and fed during 2020 and 2021 when the world was forced to stay at home.

I, also, dedicate it to Cathy, my wife who worked, tirelessly, to sample and review all my creations, be they in glass or rhyme.

Preface

My wife, Cathy, was diagnosed with shingles in the first week of March, 2020. With the knowledge that the Covid-19 virus was in the country and that shingles plays havoc with an immune system, we imposed lockdown status in our house nearly two weeks before the government imposed the same on the entire country.

Luckily, ahead of the rest of the country wanting to do the same, we were able to arrange deliveries from the supermarket and these have taken place every week since early March 2020.

I do not recall why I started down the weekly cocktail path but I am fond of a very dry vodka martini and we decided on Saturday, 14th March, a couple of martinis before dinner was a jolly good idea. Since we were in self-quarantine and we knew the rest of the country would join us in a couple of days, it was a very short leap to christen it a 'Quarantini'.

That was the start of it. The cocktails were mixed in my kitchen, next to the coffee machine, or on the deck, in the sunshine, depending on the weather and the time of year. I took photographs of the ingredients and the finished cocktails. I posted the photos on Facebook under the "Lockdown Saturday Cocktail 'Hour'" banner. The word 'Hour' was always in quotes because it was not meant to describe the length of time cocktails were taken. Sometimes it was, relatively, accurate and the cocktails were an aperitif before dinner. At other times, particularly in the late afternoon sunshine and warm summer evenings on the deck, Cocktail 'Hour' continued until well after dinner should have been taken. On one or two occasions, when the government allowed, friends came and our Lockdown Saturday Cocktail 'Hour' became a bit of an institution. If I didn't post photographs on Facebook, I would get messages from friends asking if everything was alright. After sixteen weeks, I thought I might stop the practice but I was persuaded to keep it going because it was expected and Facebook friends, from around the globe, waited to see our Saturday tipples. Sometimes I would get requests for recipes. Some of the cocktails were mixed from standard recipes but some were my own inventions and some were standard recipes but with a bit of an adjustment, here and there, to make them my own.

A couple of weeks into lockdown, I wrote my first rhyme about the situation we were in. At random intervals, others followed.

Eventually, the government relaxed the lockdown regulations but we continued with Lockdown Saturday Cocktail 'Hour', which was just as well because the regulations became unrelaxed in next to no time.

As the months progressed, vaccinations were developed and the world started to become inoculated against Covid-19. In England, unlike our inability to curtail the infection, we led the world in vaccination rollout. However, we remained locked down and so my cocktail mixing continued. When I received my first vaccination, I was inspired to develop a cocktail named, "The Vaccine". Very soon after my first vaccination, we passed the one year mark with the 'Week 52' cocktail. By this time, both Cathy and I had dates for our second vaccinations. We both considered that the second vaccination was the milestone that would bring us freedom and allow our worlds to start becoming more normal again. The date for Cathy's second vaccination was a Saturday so that was the day I mixed "The Vaccine".

I'm sure that we will miss our regular Saturday cocktails but I am, equally, sure that we will revisit some of our favourites on future weekends when we are, hopefully, no longer locked down.

I am a member of a private members' club in Soho, London. The club is called The Union. Within the club there is a backgammon club of which I am a member. Pre-pandemic, we met once a month at the club. However, when the club was closed during the first lockdown, we met on a Zoom meeting and played online once a week, on Thursdays.

When these unusual meetings began, I wrote a rhyme for my backgammon club-mates.

When the club opened its doors again, when the first lockdown ended, on 8th July 2020, I had a lunch reservation at the club and was moved to write a rhyme to mark the occasion.

At the end of summer, in late September, whilst some restrictions still existed, a few members of the backgammon club met for a face-to-face meeting; the first since February. This meeting took place at a beautiful old country pub that belongs to one of our number. I wrote a rhyme to commemorate that occasion.

These rhymes, as well as those more directly related to the Covid pandemic, are included here, interspersed chronologically, as they were written, amongst the cocktail pictures and recipes.

George Forsyth
May 2021

March 2020

An Introductory Rhyme

Everyone knows that 2020 saw the start of a deadly global pandemic,
So on March 16th, in the UK, all activities ceased, be they pleasure or academic.
We were confined to our homes and mixing with other households was against the rules.
Of course, there were detractors who thought it was all a hoax but they were just fools.

Everyone chose to get through this crisis in their own way
In the knowledge that it would all be over some faraway day.
I took to writing rhymes and mixing drinks to stop feeling too forlorn
And, in that way, Lockdown Saturday Cocktail 'Hour' was born.

Each weekend, a different cocktail would be mixed
And writing the occasional rhyme kept me transfixed
So that, for a few hours, at the very least
Worrying about the future of the world ceased.

This is my story of that terrible time told in rhyme and in glass.
I know that the passing of the old year into the new, need not see the virus pass
But to think of 2021 being the same as its predecessor makes me just too melancholic
And to continue drinking cocktails at the current rate could turn me into a serious alcoholic.

My love of the art of the mixologist and of the rhymer will not diminish
And we'll see this pandemic, successfully, through to its finish.
And I will find other, healthier, pursuits to follow but I'll be wary
To ensure that, whatever they are, they are far less sedentary.

June 2021

An Introductory Rhyme (Addendum)

Lockdown didn't end with 2020; the crisis continued unabated.
2021 started and continued with our freedom, similarly, truncated.
However, as the year progressed, vaccinations rolled out at double speed
And, to mix a new cocktail every Saturday, I decided to proceed.

So I developed more drinks and continued to mix
For another six months until June Twenty-six.
Cathy's birthday celebration would mark the end of this tradition
In the hope that, to a more normal life, we could transition.

Recipe Notes

In the cocktail recipes, the measure I used was a vodka shot glass that can be seen in most of the earlier photographs. It holds, approximately, 75 ml. This is the equivalent of, approximately, 2.6 fl. oz. or 0.3 US cup. The measure anyone else uses is down to personal choice but the ratios in the recipes should be retained. For Christmas, 2020, I was given a standard cocktail measure. You will notice when it starts to appear in the photographs. The measure is, more or less, the same as my vodka shot glass so I continued with the same recipe ratios, as before.

A number of my recipes require sugar syrup. Add 1 cup of sugar to 1 cup of water and heat slowly until the sugar has dissolved. Chill before using.

1 cup = 16 tablespoons or 8 fluid ounces

THE COCKTAILS

THE COCKTAILS

THE COCKTAILS

Week 1

QUARANTINI

- 3 x vodka
- tiny x dry vermouth

Add ice cubes and both the ingredients to a shaker. Shake vigorously until very well chilled. Strain into chilled martini glasses.
Garnish as you like. A twist of grapefruit is excellent

According to Noel Coward, who preferred a gin martini, "A perfect martini should be made by filling a glass with gin, then waving it in the general direction of Italy".

Whilst I like Noel Coward's quote very much, I prefer a vodka martini, very very dry. The mix of the words "martini" and "quarantine" was obvious, under the circumstances in March, 2020.

The usual accompaniment for a martini is either an olive or a twist of lemon. These work well with a gin martini but for a vodka martini, I prefer a twist of grapefruit.

Union Backgammon Club Lockdown Meetings

Every Thursday evening at half past five,
So as our competitive and social natures not to deprive,
We all pick up our computer or our phone
And in a Zoom Meeting, we're all in the zone.

Our regular meetings have stopped; The Club is closed
So, in our own homes, to meet, we are disposed;
There is no way any of us can take a rather nifty
To Soho and to Greek Street, Number Fifty.

We're in lounges and dens and kitchens and diners,
And if SASKIA can get Wi-Fi time, instead of her minors,
She'll join in the matches we play on the net
That, by our congenial Captain TIM, are set.

We see BRENDA and hear the glug-glug of her wine.
She's ready to play; that sound's a sure sign.
Some find the painting on her wall quite hypnotic
Others, have voiced that it looks mildly erotic!

GEN is on Zoom with, behind her, a guitar
I wonder what tunes are in her repertoire.
Last time ANDY was absent, his daughter's birthday was the reason why.
He was missed, as one of our ever-present backgammon alumni.

JERRY joins with backdrop fitting a politician
And CAROLINE too is ready for the competition
I've played both on a virtual board, and CRAWF too
But we're all eager to play, in person, at our usual rendezvous.

Always present with hints and helpful suggestions,
SEAN is there to answer all our questions.
When brother MIKE joins, they play the Grand Slams
Like other sporting siblings, the Sisters Will-e-ams.

In last week's final, was it because it's more cinematic
That NICOLE banished ALEX up to their attic?
Or just so that she could chat about him without him knowing
As, playing against RUSS, his dice he was throwing?

RUSS, for his part, looked so laid back all the way through
When, for each player, wins and losses did accrue.
After a gripping match, ALEX was crowned the champ
And so was allowed to climb back down to their base camp.

Our weekly tournaments and matches are a lot of fun
And it is great to see and chat to everyone
But, for ME, the major of my backgammon aims
Is, after a lot of matches to, finally, just once, beat JAMES.

Week 2

LONG ISLAND ICED TEA

- 1 x white rum
- 1 x vodka
- 1 x gin (citrus, if you like)
- 1 x tequila
- 1 x Grand Marnier (or similar, eg Triple Sec)
- Coca Cola

Add ice cubes and a lime wedge to a highball glass.
Add (in the order shown) the spirits and liqueur.
Top with coke (diet, if preferred) without stirring.

I had my first experience of Long Island Iced Tea, in the 1980s, at The Rusty Pelican in Newport Beach, California overlooking the marina and its luxury yachts. I could not believe the mix of spirits it contained and how drinkable and quenching it was.
It has been a firm favourite ever since.

02 April 2020 – Lockdown Begins

Thanks to a bug in a bat in a faraway land
We're all stuck inside; our freedom canned.
In strict isolation, two metres apart,
Or even further if you want to be smart.

Twenty-four / seven, not able, at all, to disperse
Is something never imagined when saying, "for better or worse".
An hour or two away is never meant to be a snub
But we can't even have a few down the pub!

For many, it's DIY or clearing the attic
During this time when our lives are so static.
We're not allowed out; we must all stay at home;
Curbed is our natural desire to roam.

No travelling is allowed, therefore, no commuters.
To chat to family and friends, we use our computers.
First timers on apps like Houseparty and Zoom
We're all learning, in this way, to brighten the gloom.

There are no deadlines, not any longer
So the desire to slob is getting stronger
We watch box sets on SKY and sometimes on Netflix
When self-isolating, that's how we get our kicks.

Amusing videos on YouTube and Instagram
Could be your neighbour with their own webcam.
The internet keeps us together, that's certainly true
But there are some sights we'd rather not view!

We all have ways to keep going under house arrest
But for us, it's easy, we are in no way, stressed,
Not like those who work all day, on the front line
With far too few respirators, to patients to assign.

Every day the politicians are on the television
To give us the statistics, in their latest revision
But it means nothing; we learn, precisely, naught
No wonder our tempers become more and more fraught.

Selected, some respected, journalists questions ask
In the hope, some answers they'll be able to unmask
But the chosen Secretary of State of the day
Very rarely has anything useful to say.

Their scripts have been written earlier that afternoon.
They tell us to stay home and, with others not to commune;
About front line professionals and how difficult is their job
With little viral protection, as fevered brows they swab.

It's not meaningless rhetoric the NHS needs, however,
It is a politician with a modicum of endeavour
Who will listen to those who know and open the communal purses
To provide equipment and funds to our doctors and nurses.

It is not millionaires at Spurs or Virgin Atlantic's Branson
Who will care for the sick, from their island or mansion
It is all those in white coats and uniforms of blue
Who, during this current crisis, will see us through.

Week 3

DARK 'N' STORMY

- good quality ginger beer
- Gosling Black Seal dark rum

Half fill a highball glass with ice cubes.

Optionally add a slice of lime.

Add ginger beer to 3/4 fill the glass.

Slowly pour rum down the inside of the glass.

A Dark 'n' Stormy is one, of two, national drinks of Bermuda. A proper one must be made using Goslings Black Seal rum; the rum of Bermuda. Less important is using Goslings ginger beer but it must be a good quality, natural ginger beer. My preference is Barritts, another Bermudian ginger beer.

When mixed correctly, it is obvious how it got its name.

Pictured (right) with a Tanqueray Sevilla gin and tonic which I served to Cathy who only likes to drink a dark 'n' stormy in Bermuda.

It is a perfect accompaniment to a Bermudian sunset, enjoyed on the pool terrace at The Reefs hotel.

06 April 2020 – Stay Indoors and Make Do

Now our PM's in hospital but it'll all be okay
Because The Queen appeared on TV to convey
That the true British Spirit will, eventually, win through
But, until then, we should all stay indoors and make do.

That's easy for her to say, some might think
Because her finances are not about on the brink
Of collapsing with prospects falling through the floor.
She has castles looked after by servants galore.

Some people need to go out to earn a crust
Which is fine; nothing further need be discussed.
But there are some selfish fools, sunbathing in the parks
Who seem to think it's a holiday; time for some larks.

They must stay at home and not congregate in groups
Otherwise, before too long, those in charge will send in the troops
To break up the parties and explain one more time
That being together outside, for now, is a crime.

Surely it is obvious, is it not common sense?
Against this infection to put up a defence
To stay away from places congested
Until everyone has been negatively tested.

If we all obey the rules to keep this virus at bay
We'll be able to venture further than our own doorway
Before too long and life, to some normality,
Will return, instead of the current total frugality.

10 April 2020 (Easter Weekend) – No Easter Celebrations This Year

The news, each day, is just getting worse;
With many more cases of sick people to nurse
And more dying; there seems to be no end
To the numbers this virus, to their graves, will send.

Stay indoors, people, do not go out
The rules are important so do not flout!
We must try our best to keep these viral germs at bay
Because the danger to life, than a sunny holiday weekend, they vastly outweigh.

The first long weekend of the year has arrived
But of all the pleasures it usually brings, we are deprived.
No holidays abroad, no long weekends by the sea;
From restaurants and bars we all must be an absentee.

No Easter church services, for those that believe
No priest or vicar their blessings to receive.
No public celebration, for fear the virus will be spread,
Of the day that Jesus returned from the dead.

No family round for Easter Sunday dinner
(For some that might make this weekend a bit of a winner)
But with no end of our curfew in sight
The future is not looking very bright.

Unlike our skies which are forecast to be full of the sun
Despite this, our fun and pleasure must all be homespun.
If you have a garden or yard, play games outside
But if not, stay home and open your windows wide.

Devise new games to play with the kids, their boredom to dilute
Or resort to old favourites like Uno, Monopoly and Trivial Pursuit.
I heard on the radio, this morning, that many are starting to keep chickens
But I'm just ploughing through the works of the author, Charles Dickens.

Now there is time for us all to do the things on our lists
For as long as the current lockdown situation persists.
When, within our own homes, we are all in containment
And, like times gone by, have to make our own entertainment.

Week 4

GIN RICKEY

- 2 x gin
- 0.5 x fresh lime juice
- soda water

Add ice to a highball, or other suitable, glass.

Add gin and lime juice.

Stir.

Add soda water to nearly fill the glass.

Garnish with a couple of thin slices of lime.

Served in the late afternoon sunshine on the deck. For ease, the gin and lime juice were mixed, into a jug, ahead of serving.

Luckily, at the beginning of 2020 before the world was locked down, we spent a couple of weeks in Malaysia. A few nights of our trip were spent in the wonderful Majestic Hotel in Kuala Lumpur.

A Gin Rickey was the complementary cocktail served, during happy hour every day, in the hotel's club lounge.

This is the same drink as we enjoyed in the colonial splendour of the hotel but, this time, served on the deck in the English sunshine.

16 April 2020 – Captain Tom

It's three weeks, now, since we were allowed outside the front door
And, at today's Downing Street briefing, we'll be told it'll be three weeks more
That we must continue our usual social gathering drought.
I'm beginning to wonder how I'll feel when I, eventually, venture out.

Staying at home has become our new norm,
T-shirts and shorts, my lockdown uniform.
In so long, I've not even buttoned a shirt
Without a daily walk, I'd be completely inert!

But there is someone I look up to and admire
To his resolve, most of us can only aspire.
For this country, he has certainly paid his dues
And now, without meaning to be, he's front page news.

His sponsorship total just keeps on increasing
As he continues his efforts, without ceasing.
He didn't seek the publicity he is now getting
As we see him walking in his picturesque setting.

Of course it is Captain Tom, of whom I am talking;
Laps around his garden, up, he is clocking
Never stopping 'til his hundredth birthday, he reaches.
It's a charitable lesson, to us all, he teaches.

Everyone who's seen him on TV is, surely, amazed
At the many millions of pounds he has raised.
Throughout the NHS it will be donated.
And an honour, in his name, must be created.

Our government must learn form this solitary old soldier
Especially, he who, the key of the public coffers is the holder.
Whatever sum, Captain Tom gives, the Exchequer should duplicate
That the NHS is being helped, to the country it would demonstrate.

Week 5

FLAMINGTINI (WATERMELON MARTINI)

- 2 x vodka
- 2 x fresh watermelon juice
- 1 x sugar syrup

Add ice cubes and all the ingredients to a shaker. Shake, vigorously, until well chilled.

Strain into chilled martini glasses.

I have a friend who is obsessed with flamingos.

The shade of pink of this martini can be varied by reducing or increasing the watermelon juice used until the desired flamingo shade is reached.

This is for you, you know who you are.

Week 6

WATERMELON CUCUMBER COOLER

- 3 x gin (citrus, if desired)
- 3 x fresh watermelon juice
- 1 x sugar syrup
- 3 x soda water
- lime (wedges)
- cucumber (thick slices)

In a shaker, muddle 2 or 3 lime wedges and 2 or 3 cucumber slices.

Add gin, watermelon juice and sugar syrup.

Shake well.

Add ice and a lime wedge to a cocktail jar or highball glass.

Strain the mix into the glass.

Add the soda water.

As you can see, from the photograph below, this was served on the deck on a warm spring evening.

It is a real thirst quencher and so easy to drink. That is why, I would always recommend it is drunk, slowly, through (stainless steel, reusable) straws.

26 April 2020 – Bleach Injection Is Not The Answer

Now April nears its end and soon it will be May
And my lockdown is now in its forty-fifth day.
With the virus, therefore, I am unlikely to be infected,
Yet, with normal life, I am still completely disconnected.

So many diary entries have been scored out
And my normal life continues in this drought.
I am not alone, of course, everybody's in the same boat
Until, for Covid-19, the experts create an antidote.

This crisis has brought many communities together
With sponsored runs in the warm sunny weather
And myriad other ways to raise money for hospital staff
Who are too busy or tired or sick to do it on their own behalf.

I'm one of the lucky ones, free of this dreadful disease
That has brought the whole world to its knees.
But, since, I have been blessed with a modicum of brains,
I will reserve the bleach for the toilets and drains.

I look to the political interviews to learn my future fate
But questions and answers are very rarely straight.
After being hated by all for so many years
It seems the only decent interviewer is Mr Morgan, first name Piers.

It's a world turned upside down and no mistake
But what will be left in this virus's wake?
How much of our old life, before it came,
Will still be there for us to reclaim?

Week 7

MOJITO

- 2 x white rum
- 2 x tsp sugar
- fresh limes aplenty
- fresh mint aplenty

Cut a lime into wedges and squeeze, lightly, into a highball glass.

Add 8 or 10 mint leaves to the glass.

Add sugar to the glass.

Muddle until the sugar is dissolved and there is a good smudge in the glass with a lovely limey minty aroma.

Add ice cubes to half fill the glass.

Add rum.

Top up with soda water and garnish with a lime wedge and a mint sprig.

Who doesn't love a Mojito? A non-rum drinker, I guess. However, if you like rum this will be a favourite, I'm sure.

Week 8

CAIPIRINHA

- 2 x cachaça
- 2 x tsp sugar
- fresh limes
- soda water (optional)

Cube half a lime and muddle with the sugar in a shaker.

Add the cachaça and stir.

Add ice cubes and a lime wedge to your desired glass.

Strain into the glass.

For a less sharp longer drink, top up with soda water.

This may be made in the glass without using a shaker.

The passion fruits were not used. Frankly, I don't know why I thought they'd add anything to the simple, standard Caipirinha.

To make the drink less sharp, the number of limes and amount of sugar can be varied.

09 May 2020 – War Against A Hidden Enemy?

Apparently, this weekend is a bank holiday one
To mark the date, in '45, when there was only a silent gun.
The war in Europe had ended; the enemy had been defeated
Returning troops, with hugs and kisses from strangers, were being greeted.

Comparisons have been drawn between then and our current plight
And that, this time round, it is a hidden enemy that we have to fight.
Is this analogy correct; can our doctors and nurses be compared
To the generation who went into battle to die, so young and so scared?

Everyone will have a view on whether this is valid or not
But in reality, it is immaterial; it matters not a jot.
In the sun, socially distanced street parties, all over the nation
Are being held, this weekend, in celebration.

Or 'meeting' with friends over Houseparty or Zoom
Instead of being all together in the same room.
Does it help to compensate for parties and weddings being postponed?
And hefty deposits, already paid, being disowned.

Businesses are closed, some never to return
For us all, this should be a major concern.
Some of our favourite brands may no longer exist
When, eventually, the virus and the lockdown are dismissed.

It seems my rhyming has taken a depressing bent
But there is no point in trying, the truth, to circumvent.
At the moment, it is just the way I'm thinking
But it will pass, I'm sure, when I start today's drinking.

When it comes to that, "everything in moderation",
Which was my late mother's favourite salutation,
Is how I approach my relationship with drinks, alcoholic
But let's see how much is needed to dispel my current thoughts, so melancholic.

Week 9

MOSCOW MULE

- 3 x vodka
- 1 x fresh lime juice
- good quality ginger beer

Half fill a highball glass with ice cubes.

Pour in the lime juice.

Pour in the vodka.

Top up with ginger beer.

Garnish with a lime wedge.

The watch in the photograph is a Russian military submariners watch. I hope it's water-proof, my mother once noted. I suggested that the Russian submariners, probably, hoped their submarine was.

Week 10

MANGO DAIQUIRI

- 2 x white rum
- 1 x fresh lime juice
- 0.5 x sugar syrup (max; mango is sweet)
- 1 or 2 mangos

Cube the mango flesh and add 4 or 5 cubes to a shaker and muddle until a good amount of juice is produced.

Add ice and the liquids and shake vigorously for a while until very chilled. (Requires more shaking than most other cocktails.)

Strain into daiquiri glasses and garnish with a small mango cube.

28 May 2020 - Dominic's Eye Test

Just when we knew we all had to stay at home
It seems we were all wrong; it was ok to roam
And visit our aged parents with wife and child
Despite having symptoms, no matter how mild.

Or having no symptoms, his account's confusing
Which is why the majority, polled, are accusing
Dominic Cummings of breaking his own rules
And taking the general public all, as fools.

He just wanted to visit his Mum and his Dad
Surely, as a good son, that can't be bad?
It would have been fine to travel to another town
If the whole country had not been tightly locked down!

No travel was allowed, "Stay At Home" was our instruction
If you don't, of our whole society, it will be the destruction!
Doesn't apply to me, thought Boris's bald headed friend
With M & D, at their country pile, some time I'll spend.

But when it was time to leave, was his eyesight impaired?
Of driving, with wife and child, in a car, he was scared.
We must make the test, if I'm blind or not,
By all driving to a local sunny beauty spot.

It's your birthday, after all, he told Mary, his wife
Why should silly lockdown change our way of life?
Let's have a family day out and sit in the sun
Come on, you two, it'll be great fun.

That was then and now he's back at his job
And, around him, swarm his loyal mob
To make up lies and back him to the hilt
Trying to prove, of rule breaking, there was no guilt.

But we're not fools; like Dominic, we are not blind
It is obvious to all that he should have resigned
So all energies are available to fight the virus, parasitical
Instead of making this all about a fight for success, political.

Week 11

STRAWBERRY BASIL MARTINI

- 1 x gin
- 1 x vodka
- 3 x fresh strawberries (hulled and halved)
- 3 x fresh basil leaves (big ones)
- 0.5 x sugar syrup

Muddle the strawberries, basil leaves and sugar syrup in a shaker.

Add ice and the spirits and shake vigorously until well chilled.

Strain into chilled martini glasses and garnish with a cut strawberry and a basil leaf.

This is a perfect late afternoon sunshine drink. The mix of strawberries and basil gives it a very refreshing tasty flavour and the mix of gin and vodka gives it a good kick when sipped slowly.

Week 12

GIN FIZZ

- 2 x gin
- 1 x fresh lemon juice
- 0.5 x sugar syrup
- soda water

Add ice cubes to a shaker and add all the still liquids. Shake, vigorously, until well chilled.

Strain into cocktail jars or highball glasses. Top with soda water and garnish with a lemon slice.

This is a very refreshing, quenching drink. The sugar syrup reduces the lemony tang a little.

Like many of our Lockdown Cocktails, it was an accompaniment to a few games of backgammon.

Week 13

COSMOPOLITAN

- 3 x vodka
- 1 x Cointreau
- 2 x cranberry juice
- 0.5 x fresh lime juice

Add ice and all the ingredients to a shaker.

Shake vigorously until very well chilled.

Strain into chilled martini glasses and serve ungarnished.

A beautiful sipping cocktail.

Nothing better to have in your hand while playing some backgammon or cribbage on the deck as the sun sets on a warm summer's day.

18 June 2020 – Lockdown Regulations Eased

Looking through the tunnel, is that light?
Is everything, now, going to be all right?
NO!, there's still a threat gripping the globe;
The viral Covid-19 killing microbe.

Shops are opening and so are the pubs
As well as our favourite Soho clubs.
Properly sanitised and 99.9% bacteria free
So their clients' good health is a guarantee.

But for complacency, there is still no room,
Back to normal, no one should presume.
Wash those hands and wear that mask
To save some lives, it's not a big ask!

Keep your distance; one metre or two
Further apart will see us through
It will be different but, to it, we'll all get used
As long as most human contact remains diffused.

Within a household, a hug doesn't get you in trouble
And with someone else you can create a bubble;
Should it be a parent or grandparent or just a friend?
The rules are still not easy to comprehend.

"Use your common sense" our Prime Minster states,
When public places open their gates,
"Which means still two metres apart" but, if you can't do that
It's ok to be closer, he says, to have a drink and a chat.

No wonder we're confused but, at least, our leader isn't Trump
We'll stop testing for it, is the brainwave of that orange coloured chump!
That way, our positive numbers will go right down
That's the goal, after all, isn't it? Can you believe that Clown!

I've seen inside all the houses of reporters and experts I need to see
Who are interviewed via Zoom or FaceTime or Skype on TV
I'm nearly back to normal because, without any prior warning,
I shouted at Piers Morgan, on television, this morning.

Baby Steps, everyone, and learn new ways to behave
That way we'll do our best to avoid a second wave.
Wear masks and don't touch anything on busses and trains
And, for the country's economy, we might start to see some gains.

Week 14

SOUTHSIDE FIZZ

- 2 x gin
- 1 x Cointreau
- 1 x lemon and lime juice (freshly squeezed)
- 0.5 x sugar syrup
- Mint leaves

Muddle about 6 mint leaves in the bottom of a shaker.

Add all liquids and stir (a lot).

Add 3 ice cubes, a twist of lemon and a thin slice of lime to a highball glass.

Strain into the glass from the shaker.

Top with soda and garnish with a mint sprig.

You can tell from the long shadows that sunset was not very far off when I served these on the deck at the end of a warm sunny day. A perfect refresher to watch the sun go down.

Week 15

CARELESS WHISPER

- 1 x tequila
- 1 x Camomilla (camomile liqueur)
- 0.5 x fresh lime juice
- 2 x pink grapefruit juice
- 0.15 x sugar syrup
- soda water

Add ice cubes and all the ingredients (except the soda water) to a shaker.

Shake vigorously until well chilled.

Nearly fill a tumbler with ice (crushed, if you like).

Strain in the mixture.

Add soda water to nearly the top.

Garnish with a fresh pink grapefruit wedge.

Drink while listening to the song (optional).

Named in memory of George Michael and created, for him by his favourite bar in Ibiza, I believe.

The Camomilla softens the acidy citrus of the lime and grapefruit juices. The lingering flavour is that of tequila.

08 July 2020 - On Being Union-ised Again

It's the day I've longed for since the doors were locked
And entry to my favourite home from home was blocked.
After so long, to London taking steps so tentative
With face mask and all other measures, preventative.
I look forward to the kitchen and bar being fully stocked.

Meeting with friends for a long lunch and a chat
Wednesday afternoons are just made for that.
If the sun is shining on the terrace rooftop
Or, like today, inside the Club if the rain starts to drop.
For as long as we're allowed, we'll be here chewing the fat.

Which is not a reflection on Carolyn's meat selection
Despite the lockdown time she still has the best connection.
In the kitchen they cook up the tastiest grub
For all the happy members of our Club.
Keeping our minds off, for a while, the Covid Infection.

It bodes well that our Club, whose sanctum we all crave,
Will be there so its members' sanity it can save
By being open, each week, for just a few days
When we're in the end of Lockdown's first phase.
As long as we're careful and there is no second wave.

Week 16

RETURN TO FOREVER

- 1 x gin
- 1 x white rum
- 0.5 x fresh lemon juice
- 2 x pineapple juice

- 1 x vodka
- 0.5 x Cointreau
- 0.5 x cranberry juice
- soda water

Add ice cubes to a shaker and add all the above (except the soda water).

Shake vigorously until well chilled.

Add a slice of fresh lime and some ice cubes to a highball glass.

Strain in the mixture.

Add soda water to nearly the top.

Play 'Romantic Warrior' by Return To Forever to accompany.

I created this cocktail to mark the return to Lockdown Saturday Cocktail 'Hour' after last Saturday's tradition was postponed, until Sunday, and this week was going to be our final Lockdown Saturday Cocktail 'Hour'. [Spoiler - It wasn't]

18 July 2020 – Lockdown Saturday Cocktail Hour

Some people have taken Lockdown Time to curb their drinking
But not me; that was never part of my thinking.
And some, but not me, drink if the day has a "Y" in it
But don't get me wrong, I am not trying to be a hypocrite.

On Thursdays, I imbibe, and on Saturday evenings too.
I'll find a bottle, a glass and my favourite corkscrew.
On Thursdays, it's with my backgammon club; we meet online
While, on Saturdays, I mix drinks that don't, usually, include wine.

Every weekend, there's Cocktail 'Hour' late on Saturday afternoon
On warm days, up on the deck, until the rising of the moon.
It started, eighteen weeks ago, with a "quarantini",
Lots of vodka, a grapefruit twist and, of dry vermouth, just a teeny.

Every Saturday, I've mixed a different cocktail to drink before dinner
Sometimes short, sometimes long but every one a winner.
It was something to look forward to; a bit of a treat
Which in those dire days, helped keep our spirits more upbeat.

In the lockdown times, I needed a marker for the day of the week.
On Thursdays, the backgammon club Zoom call made that day unique
And prompted me to get creative because two short days later
I'd be a mixologist and a cocktail waiter.

When every day was the same as the next and the one before
And with others, face to face, we had no rapport,
We promised we could do better and our whole lives we'd cleanse
So we could return to going out and meeting up with friends.

Now lockdown's eased and normality is very slowly returning
Have we forgotten the lessons we spent so many long months learning?
We still must not form a crowd for fear of furthering the infection.
We must keep socially distanced for our own, and others, protection.

Week 17

PINEAPPLE MARGARITA

- 2 x tequila
- 1 x Triple Sec (or other orange liqueur)
- 2 x pineapple juice

Add all ingredients to a shaker and stir well.

Add crushed ice to a daiquiri or martini glass.

Pour in the combined ingredients and garnish with a sprig of mint or a pineapple slice.

If desired, add a little soda water to make a long drink.

The day before I served this cocktail, 24 July 2020, was National Tequila Day.

I mixed this in recognition of that day.

The addition of pineapple juice makes for a very refreshing, fruity margarita without the 'sting' of the, regular, fresh lime juice.

Week 18

MAI TAI (and fruity option)

- 1 x white rum
- 0.5 x Triple Sec
- 0.75 x fresh lime juice

- 1 x gold rum
- 0.5 x Orgeat (almond orange syrup)

Add ice cubes and all ingredients to a shaker.

Shake vigorously until well chilled.

Half fill a tumbler with roughly crushed ice.

Pour in the shaken ingredients.

Squeeze a lime wedge and drop into the glass.

For the fruity option, top with equal amounts of fresh orange and pineapple juices.

A straight Mai Tai can be quite a potent drink and should be treated carefully.

The addition of the juices turns the straight Mai Tai into a lovely longer drink. The mix of orange and pineapple juices combines very well with the spirits.

Week 19 (Part 1)

KARLI'S KOMFORT

- 1 x Karli's strawberry and lavender gin*
- 0.5 x Triple Sec
- 1 tsp Karli's strawberry and Pimm's jam**
- soda water

Add all the ingredients to a shaker and stir until the jam is, mostly, dissolved. Add ice cubes and shake vigorously.

Add plentiful ice cubes to a tumbler and strain in the mixture.

Add an equal amount of soda water.

Garnish with a half strawberry and sprig of mint.

Lockdown had been relaxed, a little, and I served this cocktail when a couple of friends joined us on the deck on a Friday which was, until then, the hottest day in the UK ever. The temperatures were bettered by a few degrees, later in the year.

A few days earlier, we had visited our friend, Karli, in the Cotswolds. She had a plethora of fresh strawberries, living, as she did, close to the farm that supplied the Wimbledon championships. Of course, that did not happen in 2020 and Karli had acquired most of their stock.

She gave me some of the gin and jam, that she had made. The gin and jam recipes are on the next page.

I created this cocktail as a tribute.

* For Karli's strawberry and lavender gin

- 500g strawberries
- 0.5 vanilla pod
- 200g caster sugar
- 1 tsp edible dried lavender
- 800ml gin

Hull and half the strawberries and place in a wide rimmed jar.

Remove the seeds from the vanilla pod.

Stir the sugar, lavender, vanilla seeds and pod into the gin.

Pour in the gin and stir gently.

Seal the jar and leave to macerate for, at least, 2 weeks. Gently rock the jar each day to dissolve the sugar.

Strain the gin through a muslin lined fine mesh sieve into a clean bottle.

** For Karli's strawberry and Pimm's jam

- 2kg strawberries
- 40ml water
- 80ml lemon juice
- 1kg sugar
- 150ml Pimm's

Hull and half the strawberries and place in a large jam pan with water and soften on a moderate eat for 10-15 minutes.

Add the lemon juice and sugar and stir to dissolve the sugar.

Bring the mixture to the boil and boil steadily for 20-25 minutes, stirring occasionally.

Test the jam by taking a little from the pan and placing on a plate. Push your finger into it. If it, mostly, stays apart, it's ready. If not, continuing boiling for a few more minutes.

Remove from the heat and skim off any scum from the surface.

While it is still hot, stir in the Pimm's and leave for a few minutes so that the alcohol burns off.

Ladle into sterilised jars and seal.

Week 19 (Part 2)

ESPRESSO MARTINI

- 1 x vodka
- 1 x Kahlùa (or other coffee liqueur)
- 1 x espresso (decaf cos it's late)
- a little sugar syrup may be added, if required

Add ice cubes to a shaker and add all the ingredients.

Shake vigorously until very well chilled.

Strain into a martini glass.

Garnish with 3 unnecessary coffee beans, if required. (They're never required.)

After dinner, with a couple of friends, there is no better way to finish off the evening than with an ESPRESSO MARTINI. I served these on the deck, well after sunset, on the same Friday as we preceded dinner with KARLI'S KOMFORT. Under the circumstances, I didn't take very good photographs. However, it was a wonderful evening!

CHERRY FIZZ

- 1 x vodka
- 1 x Edinburgh strawberry pink pepper gin
- 1 x sour cherry juice
- 0.5 x fresh lime (squeezed)
- Prosecco

Add ice and all the still ingredients to a shaker and shake vigorously until chilled.

Add ice cubes to a cocktail jar and squeeze and drop in a lime wedge.

Pour in the contents of the shaker and top with Prosecco.

For this, my own recipe, I used strawberry pink pepper gin which is very suitable for this cocktail. However, it may not be to everyone's taste. Any gin would be perfectly acceptable for this cocktail. The hint of sour cherry flavour is what is important.

Week 21

PINA COLADA

- 1 x white rum
- 1 x coconut cream
- 2 x pineapple juice

Add ice and all the ingredients to a shaker and shake vigorously until chilled.

Fill a tumbler with crushed ice and pour in the contents of the shaker.

Garnish with a pineapple wedge.

A Classic that never goes out of fashion.

It might be better if it is served with the sound of the Caribbean Sea lapping on the shore while you watch the sun setting on the horizon.

Failing that, search for Rupert Holmes singing "Escape" on Spotify.

Week 22

CHILLI WATERMELON COOLER

- 1 x vodka
- 0.5 x triple sec
- 2 x fresh watermelon juice
- pinch of red chilli powder
- 0.25 x sugar syrup
- soda water

Blend the chilli powder with the watermelon juice and sugar syrup until smooth.

Add ice and all the ingredients to a shaker and shake vigorously until well chilled.

Add ice to a tumbler and strain in the contents of the shaker.

Top up with soda water and stir before serving.

The size of the pinch of chilli powder should vary according to taste. I served this with guests, one of whom was not fond of chilli so she had a gin fizz (see Week 12).

02 September 2020 – No Foreign Holidays for Me!

Well, it seems that 2020's summer has come and almost gone
Unless there's an Indian one waiting round the corner to come on.
Unique in everyone's lifetime, this year has been
But, at least, we've learned to keep our hands nice and clean.

We've all stayed at home or ventured only close by
Very few of us have gone anywhere that required us to fly.
Now almost everywhere you go, it's quarantine once returned,
And all usual communing, for 14 days, must be spurned.

Was it worth it just for two weeks in a sunny foreign land?
You could have stayed at home and got just as tanned;
But they say that a change is as good as a rest
So a holiday is essential to keep depression suppressed.

Good luck to those who, to sunnier climes, have fled.
The furtherest I've travelled, from home, was Beachy Head!
It is as if this year is being lived in slow motion
And I cannot wait to get into an airplane and fly over an ocean.

Visiting friends, is what I do, in other parts of the earth.
This year, of course, there's been a complete dearth
Of the travel that I love and that I plan each year
Because of the global infection that is so severe.

Let's hope 2021 brings an end to this world-wide infection.
Let's hope there will be a vaccine to give us all protection
So life can return to normal and we can, again, be free
To venture, far and wide, across land and sea.

Week 23

COCONUT RUM JULEP

- 2 x white rum
- 0.5 x fresh lime juice
- 1.5 x coconut cream
- 1 x sugar syrup
- mint sprigs

Muddle mint and sugar syrup in a shaker.

Add rum, lime juice and coconut cream and shake vigorously.

Add ice and shake again until well chilled.

Half fill a tumbler with crushed ice and strain in the mixture.

Garnish with a sprig of mint.

"Julep" simply means a sugary syrup drink. Mint Julep, made with bourbon, is the most well known but this rum coconut version is a delicious, very more-ish sipping drink.

Week 24

CUCUMBER DIRTY MARTINI

- 2.5 x gin
- 0.5 x dry vermouth
- 0.25 olive juice
- cucumber juice
- pinch of salt

Cube the cucumber and liquidise with the salt. Sieve into a container and set aside the cucumber juice.

Add ice, gin, vermouth and olive juice to a mixing glass and stir well for 30 seconds.

Add a splash (to taste) of cucumber juice and stir again.

Strain into a chilled martini glass and garnish with a cucumber sliver and an olive.

The addition of cucumber juice takes the edge off the savoury flavour of a dirty martini.

The ratios of all four liquids can be varied until the ideal flavour is obtained. The measures, here, are simply a guide.

The mixture can be shaken instead of stirred, if desired.

30 September 2020 - Union Backgammon Club At The Lantern

This year, on the last day of September
A pub belonging to a Union member
Hosted an evening of games and fun
When, by The Backgammon Club, it was overrun.

We were at the 17th century Lantern Inn
Which came with ghosts, resident within.
Our host was the lovely Andy Blake
And places on the backgammon ladder were what was at stake.

Tim and Derek and Andy and James
Were all in the mood to play some games
And so were Jerry and George and the only girl, Brenda,
Who had glasses of Amaretto on her agenda.

None of us held back, when it came to the bar
And the buffet was delicious with Chef Martin the star,
Who, along with Joe, made sure our glasses were always filled
With something that had been brewed or fermented or distilled.

We ate and drank and played games well into the night
With our Skipper, Tim, keeping score, while he was still able to write
And when, eventually, it was decided that it was time we retired
"We'll all have a nightcap", suggested Martin, "that's what's required".

A signature tipple at The Lantern is chilled XO Café
So shots, for all, were poured without delay
But not for Brenda who, of the coffee flavoured tequila was unsure,
So she stuck to a few more glasses of her favourite almond liqueur.

We were all staying at The Lantern, in various locations,
Adhering, more or less, to all the current Covid regulations.
I slept with Cathy, my wife, above the pub, in the flat.
In the second bedroom, was Brenda, in this beautifully restored habitat.

Derek was sensible and went home, which wasn't too far.
Jerry was in one of the bunks built like a railway couchette car.
And after the nightcaps had done a few rounds
The other boys went off to a yurt, installed in the grounds.

The next morning, breakfast orders were taken
Delivered in rolls the size of doorsteps and, mostly, involving bacon.
We sat and ate and drank coffee and juice
And mused over the previous night's brain cell abuse.

James told how he'd called it a night before he went asunder
And, without anyone knowing, had done a "tactical chunder".
Tim admitted that, during the night in the yurt, on his mattress on the floor
He'd needed to go out for a wee but he couldn't find the door.

Eventually he found the exit and fell out onto the grass,
However, from describing the next few minutes, I think we should pass.
The next morning, it took some time before our esteemed Skipper
Could claim that he was feeling suitably chipper.

Later, James kept us laughing when he told us of the time his boat he was towing
Down, through France, to Portugal, but the route he wasn't knowing,
So he relied on his satnav but in finding the best route it fell a bit short
And James and his boat ended up in an Andorran ski resort.

And that's the story of the Union Backgammon Club's stay at The Lantern Inn
A wonderful time so it didn't matter if, your games, were a loss or a win.
But I'll remember, specifically, one of my games
Because, finally, at last, I managed to beat James!

Week 25

AGUA DE VALENCIA

- 1 x gin
- Cava
- medium pinch of castor sugar

- 1 x vodka
- 2 x fresh orange juice
- 3 or 4 pieces of finely diced orange peel

Add ice to a shaker.

Add all the above ingredients (except the Cava) and stir well until the sugar is dissolved.

Shake until well chilled.

Quarter fill a chilled wine glass with crushed, or cubed, ice.

Place a thin slice of orange on top of the ice.

Strain in the mixture from the shaker.

Top up with Cava.

I first sampled this in its Spanish city of origin. This is an extremely refreshing drink and very, very easy to drink quickly in the sun.

However, beware, it is, deceptively, strong.

Week 26

SEA BREEZE

- 1 x vodka
- 2 x cranberry juice
- 0.5 x triple sec
- 1 x grapefruit juice

Half fill a tall glass with ice cubes.

Add all the ingredients to the glass and stir until the outside of the glass is chilled to the touch.

Garnish with a slice of lime.

The Sea Breeze is a favourite of an American friend of mine. I added triple sec to the standard recipe because all fruity cocktails are better with a little triple sec.

It's always good to have a bottle of triple sec in the liquor cabinet because you just never know when......

PALOMA

For the salted grapefruit cordial....

- 3 x ruby red grapefruits
- 1 x cup sugar
- 0.25 x cup fresh lime juice
- 0.25 x cup water
- 1.5 x tsp salt

The day before, bury the peel from 1 grapefruit in the sugar in a pint glass. Cover and refrigerate for 24 hours. Then......

Add the juice from all the grapefruits, lime juice, water and salt and shake or stir until the sugar is dissolved.

Remove the peel and refrigerate.

This cocktail was suggested to me by a friend.

It's a bit of a faff but the resulting drink is well worth it.

The cordial will keep, chilled, for another occasion.

For the cocktail.....

- 2 x blanco tequila
- 1 x salted grapefruit cordial
- 0.25 x Campari
- 0.75 x fresh lime juice

Add ice to a shaker.
Add all the ingredients and shake vigorously until well chilled.
Half fill your chosen glass with ice and strain in the mixture.
Garnish with a grapefruit twist.

Week 28

SEX ON THE BEACH

- 2 x vodka
- 1 x peach schnapps
- 2 x orange juice
- 2 x cranberry juice

Half fill a highball glass with ice.

Add vodka, peach schnapps and orange juice to the glass and stir.

Slowly pour over the cranberry juice.

Garnish with a fresh orange wedge.

It was a cold, damp English autumn evening. This fruity little Classic helped to brighten it.

Usually, I fly off for some sun towards the end of the year but 2020 is different. Memories and tastebuds are all I have this year.

Week 29

NEGRONI

- 1 x Campari
- 1 x Gin
- 1 x Vermouth Rosso
- orange

Add ice to a tumbler and pour in the ingredients. Stir.

Garnish with a small orange wedge.

A simple and delicious sipping drink. Each of the ingredients have a very strong flavour but when stirred together equally, their individual strengths are softened.

Ideal for a cold autumn evening accompanying a friendly backgammon match.

Week 30

ZOMBIE

- 1 x dark rum
- 1 x fresh lime juice
- 1 x tsp grenadine
- 1 x white rum
- 4 x pineapple juice

Add ice to a shaker and pour in the rums and fruit juices.

Shake vigorously until well chilled.

Nearly fill a highball glass with ice and strain from the shaker.

Drop in a thin orange wedge.

Slowly drizzle the grenadine over a couple of floating ice cubes.

Served on Halloween 2020. No other cocktail seemed suitable.

When the grenadine is drizzled over the floating ice cubes it slowly falls like dripping blood. That, of course, is why it's in the recipe. As well as adding another flavour.

Under normal circumstances, on Halloween, we meet with a couple of Bermudian chums for dinner in St George's, Bermuda. Not, however, in 2020.

I, initially, thought that a mint sprig would be a suitable garnish. I was wrong. Like coffee beans in an espresso martini, completely unnecessary.

01 November 2020 – U-Turn to Lockdown Part Two

Now we're locked down, again, for the next four weeks.
We all tune in and listen, as the Prime Minister speaks.
He tells us there is no option because infections have not decreased
And he wants our families to be all together for the annual Christmas feast.

However, if he'd listened to the scientists who advise him
The situation we're in might not be quite so grim.
Shutdown and stop all contact, months earlier, they advised
But it seems that Boris, their expert opinions, despised.

"Eat out to help out" was what he had said we should do
And, together, this unprecedented crisis, we'll all get through.
For the downward economy and our insanity there was a little respite
But, in reality, at the end of the tunnel, there was no light.

This is how we must live; we must not drop our guard;
We've had months of practice so it shouldn't be too hard
To stay in our household or in a pre-defined bubble
And with the pubs being shut there shouldn't be any trouble.

This government has U-turned so often, there is rubber all over the road.
It's showered out billions, for an app, to companies that couldn't even code.
We can only hope that it'll turn, once more, and decide to feed
Children who have nothing, except for food, a desperate need.

07 November 2020 – USA Election

In the USA, the tension, recently high, is abating
As, the world, the Presidential election result, is awaiting.
It is expected that the White House will, again, be blue
Which will be a welcome change from the current orangey-red hue.

They're not very quick at counting, our American friends
But those Democratically biased, know it will pay dividends
And they will see their man, in January, safely inaugurated
When Donald John Trump, the Oval Office, has vacated.

But what havoc can he reap before his tenure is completed?
Will we be able to count the number of insults he has tweeted?
Will all his friends fall away like leaves from a tropical frangipani?
And the only one left by his side will be his faithful Rudy Giuliani.

One thing, we can all agree, regarding his departure, as a surety
Is that he will not go quietly and simply fade into obscurity.
We can expect even more lawsuits, by his team, filed
And, perhaps, some against him for the laws he has defiled.

Let's confine "The Trump Years" to the history book
And move forward with a more promising outlook
For the new administration, their polices to divest,
And hope that Trump's final legacy isn't civil unrest.

Week 31

SAKETINI

- 1 x gin OR vodka
- 1 x good quality sake
- 0.25 x dry vermouth
- cucumber or lemon

Add ice to a shaker. Add the ingredients and shake, or stir, until well chilled. Strain into a chilled martini glass.

Garnish with a thin slice of cucumber or a twist of lemon peel.

We decided to try both. A gin saketini (garnished with cucumber) and a vodka saketini (garnished with a lemon twist). We assumed we'd each have one, then try the other. However, I stuck with the vodka saketini and Cathy stayed with the gin saketini.

Each to their own.

60 | My Covid Time in Glass & Rhyme

14 November 2020 – Departures on Both Sides of The Atlantic

That's it; he's gone; in charge, he is no more
He's left the building so bolt the door.
His return will never be wanted or required
His tenure, in decision making, has expired.

No more Dominic Cummings in No. 10; Carrie said, "go!"
It wasn't Boris, if you believe what you read in the tableaux,
Who issued the marching orders but Ms Symonds, mother of his latest child.
There was a falling out with the three of them that couldn't be reconciled.

Now let's cross the Atlantic and to the House that is White,
Where the current President will not be leaving without a fight.
His remaining there, by the American people, is not wanted
But, it seems, he plans to remain and continue, in office, undaunted.

Trump, once Republican, now seems to be veering towards autocracy.
Waging his own, personal, war against American democracy.
A war which, of course, like the election, he will not win
So, on January the twentieth, the healing process will begin.

A healing process for America and, hopefully, across the globe
With 2021 being the year we beat this deadly Coronavirus microbe.
We will look back on the dark cloud of a year that 2020 has been
And forward to the sliver lining which is the news of a healing vaccine.

Week 32

GIMLET

For the lime syrup......

- 4/5 x limes, zest and juice
- 200g caster sugar
- water

Put the lime zest into a saucepan.

Measure about 100ml of juice into a jug and top up with water to about 150ml.

Pour the liquid into the pan with the caster sugar and heat, gently without boiling, until the sugar is dissolved. The quantities of limes and sugar may vary. The syrup should be sweet, but not too sweet with a strong, but not too strong, lime flavour.

Strain into a jug and leave to cool.

For the cocktail......

- 2 x gin
- 2 x lime syrup

Add ice to a shaker and add the gin and lime syrup. Shake, or stir, until well chilled.

Strain into a chilled martini glass and squeeze the juice of half a lime on top.

Garnish with a thin slice of lime.

A longer, more refreshing, variation, shown on the right, contains half the quantities of gin and lime syrup in a highball glass with lots of ice and topped up with soda water.

This is not one of the regular weekly cocktails.

I created this cocktail following a conversation with members of the Union Backgammon Club. This is a suitable, sipping accompaniment to a winter's backgammon match or, indeed, just a quiet evening beside a roaring fire.

THE UNION

- 1.5 x gin
- 0.5 x Vermouth Rosso
- 0.25 x Montelobos Mezcal
- 0.25 x triple sec
- 0.25 x lime syrup

Montelobos Mezcal has a distinctly smokey finish. This helps to give The Union its unique flavour. However, if this is not to your liking, substitute the mezcal with good quality silver tequila.

To make the lime syrup, refer to the Gimlet recipe on page 62.

Half fill a tumbler with ice cubes.

Add all the ingredients and stir well until nicely chilled.

Garnish with an orange wedge.

Week 33

HURRICANE

- 1 x dark rum
- 1 x sugar syrup
- 1 orange (juiced)
- 1 x tsp grenadine

- 1 x white rum
- 1 passion fruit
- 1 lime (juiced)

Add ice to a shaker then add the rums.

Scoop the flesh and seeds from the passion fruit and add to the shaker.

Add the orange and lime juices along with the sugar syrup and grenadine to the shaker.

Shake vigorously until well chilled.

Nearly fill a hurricane glass (a tall highball glass will do instead) with ice and double strain from the shaker.

Garnish with an orange wedge.

Winter in England is not quite Mardi Gras in New Orleans but this is the taste of Mardi Gras, wherever you are.

Week 34

YAAKA HULA HICKEY DULA

- 1.5 x dark rum
- 1.5 x dry vermouth
- 1.5 x pineapple juice

Add ice and all the ingredients to a shaker.

Shake vigorously until well chilled.

Add ice (cubed or crushed) to a tumbler or cocktail jar and strain the ingredients into the glass.

Garnish with a wedge of orange.

Named after an Hawaiian love song recorded in 1916 by Al Jolson.

Playing the song is a very suitable accompaniment to this cocktail.

30 November 2020 – Lockdown Relaxation for Christmas

The second English Lockdown is soon coming to an end
But it doesn't mean that, again, we can meet a friend
Or have the usual gatherings that happen at this time of year
Because we must follow the rules laid down for our tier.

The rules are confusing and difficult to understand
But, basically, all socialising still has to be canned
Except in the top two tiers where in groups of six
In some circumstances, we are allowed to mix.

But not indoors, if we're located in tier number two
And meeting others from different households just won't do.
We can go to a pub with others in our bubble, if that should appeal
But only if we all have a substantial meal.

Of course, come Christmas week, all the rules are changed
And it's ok to meet those, with whom all year, we've been estranged
And form an exclusive Christmas Bubble from households up to three
To eat and drink and exchange gifts around the tree.

Even before then, the Minister for Health has stated,
Some old people may already have been inoculated
So they can move around, confidently, within their local bubble
But it's not going to be the over eighties that cause the trouble.

I think it will be obvious and can easily be predicted
That, come January, many more people will have been afflicted
And we'll look back and wonder, was it worth the additional infections
As we await the call to fall in line for our immunising injections.

Week 35

RUSTY NAIL

- 2 x scotch whisky
- 1 x Drambuie

Add 2 or 3 ice cubes to a whisky glass and pour in the ingredients.

Stir and garnish with a lemon twist.

It was St Andrew's Day earlier in the week so a Scottish cocktail seemed appropriate.

A blended Scotch whisky is suitable.

Some aficionados might baulk at me using 'The Glenlivet' which is a lovely single malt.

09 December 2020 – The Vaccine Has Arrived

It's two weeks since we were told the MRHA had made their decision.
We've seen the Secretary of State for Health in tears on national television
Because the vaccines have arrived and inoculations have commenced
So, around the country, huge sighs of relief can be sensed.

Starting next month, when the Christmas celebrations end
We'll wait for a phone call or a text or an email to be penned
That will give us the news, for so long, we've been awaiting
That we will soon, in mass inoculations, be participating.

We must praise the scientists who have struggled, without rest
And who have, certainly, shown the human race at its very best
As, in labs around the world, wearing their protective white coats
They have used all their skills to perfect the Coronavirus antidotes.

But, although not locked down, the country is still tiered
Because the infection has far from disappeared
So we all need to remain calm so we stay uninfected
Until the whole country, with vaccine, has been injected.

Other countries too, around the world, must follow our lead
Before, for everyone, normality can finally be decreed.
And so we can all feel happy to travel and interact
The way we did, before, with this virus, the world was attacked.

Week 36

BICYCLETTE

- 0.5 x Campari
- 2 x dry white wine

Add 2 or 3 ice cubes to a wine glass and pour in the ingredients.

Stir and garnish with a lemon wedge.

An unusual mix of ingredients in this no fuss cocktail.

I know that Campari is not to everyone's taste but this is a very easy and pleasant-to-drink cocktail.

19 December – Feed The Children and Christmas Is Cancelled

Well that, very nearly, was the year, that was!
I wonder what will be in our letters to Santa Claus.
World Peace and, for All, Love and Affection?
Or, very simply, an end to this global infection?

I know what I wish for as 2020 concludes;
It is a change to peoples' attitudes
Towards others, less fortunate than themselves
Who find it difficult to pay for food from the shelves.

Keeping their children fed, over the festive season,
To being alive, is their only reason.
Yet, some, who have much more than they will ever require,
Ignore the fact that others' straits are so dire.

The circumstances of this year have proved
How far, from reality, some are removed.
This year, especially, it has been so easy to be critical
Of those, whose decisions have been, obviously, political.

Let's hope that, this Christmas, common sense will prevail
And we're not tempted, with others, too wassail
Until the deadly infection has been vaccinated into submission
And there is, no longer, a risk of infectious transmission.

Then at 4:20pm

And now, Tier Four has been invented
As Boris, our PM, has just presented.
Christmas is cancelled; apart from one day
But, at home, everyone should still stay.

There is a new Covid virus mutation
That has caused our festivities' truncation.
Against it, we must put up every defence
Which is what we've been doing all year, if we had any sense!

Week 37

SIDECAR

- 1 x cognac
- 0.5 x lemon juice
- 0.5 x triple sec
- Angostura bitters

Add ice and all the ingredients, except the bitters, to a shaker.

Shake vigorously until well chilled.

Add one drop of bitters to a chilled martini glass and strain in the contents of the shaker.

A delicious sipping drink ideal for a cold December evening but just as suitable for a warm summer's day.

Week 38

BERMUDIAN SUNSET

- 1.5 x Gosling Gold Seal rum
- 0.5 x triple sec
- 2 x drops Angostura Bitters

- 0.5 x Captain Morgan Spiced Gold rum
- 1 x tsp Grenadine
- Orange juice

This is another of my own inventions but with a nod to a couple of standards.

For the first time in 6 years, we've not been able to travel to Bermuda to meet our friends and spend some time on this beautiful island.

Add ice and the rums and triple sec to a shaker.

Shake vigorously until well chilled.

In a hurricane glass, drop in the bitters.

Add 3 or 4 ice cubes and a teaspoon of Grenadine.

Pour in the contents of the shaker and top up with fresh orange juice.

01 January 2021 – Brexit Has Happened

So here we are on January the First,
And now that 2020 has done its worst,
We hope that from the virus we'll become estranged
But, in our hearts, we know that nothing has changed.

It's just another new day, like any other before.
The world is still in the grips of a deadly spore.
The virus knows not of this being a New Year.
There are no new rules to which it has to adhere.

But we wake, today, with new rules governing our land
The enormity of which, I'm sure, very few understand.
When you need a new passport, it's colour will be blue
But crossing borders, with it, will not be easier, hitherto.

Now separate from our neighbours across the Channel and Irish Sea
The advantages of which have never been clear to me.
"We'll get our sovereignty back", was the Brexiteers' shout,
And "standing alone we'll be better off"; of that they had no doubt.

However, there are two things that should bring us cheer
As, on this day, we look forward to a brand New Year.
Global vaccination will lift us from our current slump
And, on January Twenty, America will be rid of Donald Trump!

Week 39 (and now into 2021)

QUEEN'S PARK HOTEL SUPER COCKTAIL

- 1 x white rum
- 0.5 x vermouth rosso
- 0.25 x sugar syrup
- 7 x dash Angostura Bitters

- 1 x gold rum
- 0.5 x lime juice (freshly squeezed)
- 0.1 x Grenadine syrup

Add ice and all the ingredients to a shaker.

Shake vigorously until well chilled.

Strain into a chilled martini glass and garnish with a lime twist.

I adapted a recipe which itself was adapted from a recipe that appeared in *"If Crab No Walk: A Traveller in the West Indies"*, a book written in 1932 by British travel writer Owen Rutter. He wrote about the Queen's Park Hotel in Port of Spain, Trinidad, whose Long Bar served the Queen's Park Hotel Super Cocktail.

05 January 2021 – A New Year; A New Lockdown

Now we're locked down again; what a surprise!
Couldn't have seen that coming, unless you've got eyes
And half a brain and a modicum of common sense.
For this government's decisions, there is no defence.

Let people meet up at Christmas, what can go wrong?
At Christmas time, together, they all belong.
Not in 2020, you blonde-headed buffoon,
Everyone could see it was far too soon.

And now, for your mistakes, we're all paying the price
Because you disregarded the experts' advice.
Lockdown in September was what you were told
But, no, you allowed infections to continue, uncontrolled.

You couldn't 'cancel' Christmas, your popularity would suffer
So, now, all our lives have to be tougher.
But your labouring under a gross misapprehension
If you think, after this, your popularity will be in the ascension.

What was required, a year ago, was some proactivity
Which would have helped to reduce our time in captivity.
Instead, we'll all wait for our turn for the immunising injection.
How long is it until the next General Election?

Week 40

AUSSIE RULES

- 1 x white rum
- 0.5 x dry vermouth
- 2 x dash Angostura Bitters

- 1 x vodka
- 0.75 x lime juice (freshly squeezed)
- Sprite / 7-Up

Add ice to a tumbler and pour in the rum, vodka, vermouth and lime juice.

Stir well.

Dash in the bitters and top up with, either, Sprite or 7-Up.

My alcoholic version of the Australian non-alcoholic classic, Lemon Lime and Bitters.

Week 41

ROCK BEAUTY

- 1.5 (3) x Gosling Gold Seal rum
- 0.5 (1) x Triple Sec
- 1.5 (3) x Giffard Crème Pamplemousse Pink Grapefruit Liqueur

- Gosling Black Seal rum

The ratio of the ingredients is shown in brackets.

Add ice and the ingredients to a shaker and shake vigorously until well chilled.

Pour into a chilled coupe glass.

Drizzle a couple of drops of Gosling Black Seal rum on top.

I invented this cocktail as a tribute to the beautiful pink sands of Bermuda. It is named after the room we stay in, annually (except 2020), at The Reefs Hotel on South Shore Road, Bermuda.

19 January 2021 - The Trump Era Ends on My Birthday

After eleven months of letting all travellers cross our border,
Finally, the government has seen sense and issued a long-awaited order.
To anyone not holding a negative test, the border will be firmly closed
So, to Covid-19 infection, every UK resident will become less exposed.

Around the country, centres have been set up for mass inoculation.
Therefore, of Covid related infections, we should start to see a cessation.
Should January 2021 be the month, also, to start celebrations, albeit stilted?
Have the odds, of a return to some form of normality, in our favour been titled?

Certainly tomorrow, there are many reasons to celebrate
Because, in our calendars, January 20th 2021 is a very special date.
Across the Atlantic, it will be the end of a presidency, so despotic
And gradually, the United States, we hope, can begin to become less chaotic.

Closer to home, another ending, on the calendar, is displayed.
Tomorrow is the date on which I begin the final year of my seventh decade.
This time, last year, I looked to the future with joy and expectation;
Of these dark times ahead, I did not have any anticipation.

Twelve months on, despite the year we've had, I'm positive still
Although I know, to get back to normality, will be a struggle uphill
But in our efforts being worthwhile, we must all have belief
So that, along with our American cousins, we can let out a huge sigh of relief.

Week 42

Kingscote Kocktail

- Cognac
- Angostura Bitters
- English Sparkling wine or French Champagne
- Sugar cube

Drop a sugar cube into a champagne flute.

Add a few drops of bitters and allow them to soak into the sugar.

Pour in cognac so it covers the sugar cube.

Top up with your chosen chilled wine.

A celebration of the two major events that happened on Wednesday 20th January. In America, a new president and, in England, my 69th birthday.

Really a champagne cocktail but, instead of French champagne, I used sparkling English wine from the Kingscote Vineyard which is 5 minutes from our front door.

Week 43

ALICE SPRINGS

- 1.5 x gin
- 0.5 x orange juice
- 0.5 x tsp Grenadine
- Soda water

- 0.25 x triple sec
- 0.5 x lime juice
- 3 x drops Angostura bitters

Add ice cubes to a shaker and pour in the orange juice, lime juice, grenadine, angostura bitters, triple sec and gin and shake vigorously until well chilled.

Add a few ice cubes to a highball glass and pour in the contents of the shaker.

Top up with soda water and garnish with an orange slice.

As a tribute to all my Australian friends on Australia Day, last Tuesday, 26 January, this is my version of this very Australian sounding cocktail.

02 February 2021 - Groundhog Day

It's Groundhog Day today, which is when a rodent named Phil
Is awoken at dawn for his annual predicting drill.
As he emerged from his burrow, only one question was asked
Can he see his shadow that the early morning sun has cast?

His followers await to see what future his prediction will bring.
Will they have a long cold winter or an early sunny spring?
Because that is the extent of his forecasting ability
For which, he is garnered with much credibility.

It is believed that, if his shadow, the little fella sees
Six more weeks of a cold winter, he guarantees.
But if, his shadow, he completely disregards
An early spring is, definitely, on the cards.

Today, we are told, he predicted the former,
So, more winter will prevail before it gets warmer.
Perhaps there's more to his skill than meets the eye
Because, to our lives at moment, his prediction can, surely, apply.

Week 44

VENEZUALAN MANHATTAN

- 2 x Diplomático Reserva Exclusiva rum
- 1 x sweet vermouth
- 2 x dash Angostura bitters
- 1 x dash orange bitters

Add ice and all the ingredients to a shaker and stir until well chilled.

Strain into a chilled coupe glass.

Garnish with a glacé cherry.

A Manhattan is, of course, traditionally made with rye whiskey or Bourbon. This, excellent, Venezuelan rum mixes very well with the other ingredients to put a very acceptable slant on the traditional Manhattan.

Hint: do not use all your rum to make this cocktail. Diplomático Reserva Exclusiva rum is a delicious sipping rum, straight up or on the rocks.

13 February 2021 – My First Vaccination

Yesterday, I received a letter from the NHS
Its content, I'm sure you'll be able to guess.
With excitement, I read the words, long awaited;
It was my turn to make an appointment to be vaccinated!

On the website, I was asked to choose a date.
I picked the next day, I didn't want to wait.
This morning I drove to the vaccination centre
And stood in a socially distanced line waiting to enter.

With face mask on and hands properly sanitised,
I'm not sure I've been anywhere quite so organised.
I got to the front of the line in no time at all
As everybody, happily, followed the correct protocol.

Then it was done, in the blink of an eye
And I find it difficult to quantify
The feeling of downright elation
I feel after all these months of isolation.

Now, I'll wait patiently for my second dose of medication
In the hope that, by then, there will be a cessation,
To all the shielding and lockdown measures
And we can, once again, partake in life's wider pleasures.

Week 45

QUEEN'S PARK SWIZZLE

- 2 x white rum
- 0.25 x Muscovado sugar syrup
- 12/15 x fresh mint leaves

- 1 x lime juice (freshly squeezed)
- 3 x dash Angostura Bitters
- Soda Water

Muddle mint leaves and rum in the base of a highball glass.

Raise the bruised leaves up and around the inside of the glass to coat it with mint oils.

Add ice and the other ingredients to the glass and stir well.

Garnish with a lime wedge.

A Trinidadian version of the Cuban Mojito. The dark Muscovado sugar is, really, the only difference. Next time, I will be tempted to make it with a decent dark rum.

Week 46

FIERY MULE

- 1 x Fireball (cinnamon whiskey)
- pineapple juice
- 2 x ginger beer
- freshly squeezed lime juice

Add ice to a cocktail tumbler.

Add Fireball and ginger beer to the glass.

Add a splash of pineapple juice and a splash of lime juice.

Garnish with a lime wedge.

Fireball may be an acquired taste. As an ice-cold small shot, it is wonderful.

Diluting with ginger beer makes it a little more gentle on the palate. The mix of cinnamon and ginger flavours is relieved, slightly, with the addition of the splashes of pineapple and lime juices.

24 February 2021 – Lockdown Easing Planned (Again)

Our Prime Minster was on TV again a couple of evenings ago
Telling us when lockdown will end but we have to take it slow.
First the young children can get back to their school
Because the virus doesn't infect them, as a rule.

Some students, too, will return to their studies
But will not be allowed to socialise with their buddies
And no sitting and learning together in a lecture hall
Singular practical work is the only allowed protocol.

Then, at the end of March, we'll be able to get out of the house
But there won't be any shops open in which we can browse.
They are not allowed to open until April has begun
When we can, also, sit in a pub garden, in the sun.

On a roof terrace in Soho, you'll find me, if the weather's fine
With friends, numbering under six, waiting to dine.
And, rest assured, that I'm pulling no punches
When I say there will also be quite a few lunches.

But until May the 4th, I'll be careful when I'm out and about
And there will not be any rules that I will, knowingly, flout
Because May the 3rd is when I go for my second vaccination
Which will signal the end of this Covid-imposed time of stagnation.

Week 47

SINGAPORE SLING

- 1 x gin
- 0.25 x Grand Marnier
- 4 x pineapple juice
- 1 x tsp Grenadine

- 0.5 x cherry brandy
- 0.25 x Dom Benedictine
- 0.5 x lime juice (freshly squeezed)
- 1 x dash Angostura bitters

Add ice and all ingredients to a shaker.

Shake vigorously until well chilled.

Strain into a poco grande glass and garnish with a cherry.

A version of the original recipe developed by Ngiam Tong Boon in the Long Bar at Raffles Hotel, Singapore in 1915.

Week 48

BLACK RUSSIAN

- 1.5 x vodka
- 0.5 x Kalhua coffee liqueur

Half fill a whiskey glass with crushed or cubed ice.

Add the vodka then add the Kalhua.

Wait a few seconds for the drink to chill then serve.

Usually served as a nightcap at the end of the day. However, this is a very pleasant drink to sip, slowly, throughout the evening.

Week 49

KIR ROYALE

- Champagne / Prosecco / Sparkling White Wine
- 1 x tbsp Crème de Cassis
- frozen blackberry

Pop a frozen blackberry into a champagne flute and add the crème de cassis. Top up with the chilled wine.

A very popular aperitif that is suitable at any time of the evening.

Week 50

APPLE CIDER MULE

- 2 x vodka
- 4 x ginger beer
- 2 x apple cider
- lime juice

Add lots of ice to a Moscow Mule mug.

Add the vodka and cider.

Squeeze in the juice of half a lime and top up with the ginger beer.

It makes all the difference serving it in copper mule mugs. They keep the drink chilled and the outside remains frosted until it's finished.

And, of course, it looks so much better. Unfortunately, we didn't have them when I made Moscow Mules way back in Week 9.

25 March 2021 – Lockdown First Anniversary

So that's it, we've now been locked down for a year;
A full twelve months of isolation, so austere.
There's been times when, of light, there was glimmer
But, before it got brighter, it just grew dimmer.

Around the world, some people have been rebelling.
On tales of hoaxes and micro-chips they've been dwelling
While the rest of us wait, quietly, for the crisis cessation
And look forward to the plans of global vaccination.

If we're good, here in England, we'll soon be allowed outside
But there are so many rules by which we all have to abide.
If we don't, we'll be locked down again, for sure
Which is something that none of us want to endure.

As a population, we are all going to be tested;
We must not meet in numbers that gets places congested.
In twos and threes is fine and remember the "rule of six"?
That controlled the number of friends with whom we could mix.

Monday April 12 is the date when lives can change
To meet with five friends, outdoors, we can arrange.
It's weather dependent but I've booked my seat
At a table for lunch on a terrace in old Greek Street.

Will that date herald the beginning of restrictions reduced?
Will we be denied entry, unless a vaccination card is produced,
To pubs and clubs and our old usual haunts?
Or when we go to dine in our favourite restaurants.

The old "normal" is gone; a thing of the past
To get used to the new one, is what we'll be asked.
So get vaccinated and carry the card as proof
Then we can all meet in numbers, safely, under one roof.

Week 51

SURFRIDER

- 1.5 x vodka
- 2 x orange juice (freshly squeezed)
- Lime juce

- 1 x sweet vermouth
- 1 x tsp Grenadine

Add ice, the juice of half a lime and all the other ingredients to a shaker.

Shake vigorously until well chilled.

Strain the contents into a wine glass and garnish with a half slice of orange.

This became a firm favourite and we revisited this delicious refreshing drink, a lot, throughout the summer.

Week 52 (First Anniversary)

LONG GIN AND FRENCH

- 1 x gin
- Soda water
- 1 x dry vermouth

Half fill a high ball glass with cubed ice.

Add the gin and vermouth and stir until chilled.

Top up with soda water and garnish with lemon peel and a sprig of mint.

One year ago, exactly, we started this tradition

Which has continued, every week, without intermission.

However, back then, I never would have guessed

That a first anniversary rhyme would have to be addressed.

10 April 2020 – Outside Dining Allowed

This weekend is filled with excitement and crossed fingers
Because Monday sees the easing of restrictions; but some doubt lingers,
That, after all this time, something is bound to go wrong.
But the whole country hopes there's nothing that, lockdown, will prolong.

A midday train to London on Monday is top of my to-do list.
The hope is that it restarts a part of my life that I've long since missed.
A convivial lunch to discuss current affairs and less important matters
Amidst glasses of fine wines and chef's most deliciously filled platters.

The Union roof terrace is, of course, Monday's final destination.
Although socially distanced, there's bound to be a celebration
When we toast the re-opening, and the shutters being taken down,
Of our home from home in the West End of our beloved London Town.

Week 53

MOJITO ROYALE

- 2 x white rum
- 1 x tsp sugar
- mint leaves

- 0.5 x lime juice
- Champagne / Prosecco / Sparkling White Wine

Muddle about a dozen mint leaves in a highball glass with rum, lime juice and sugar.

Add plentiful ice cubes and top up with the sparkling wine.

Garnish with a lime wedge, if desired.

Simply a regular Mojito with the, usual, soda water replaced by your sparkling wine of choice. This gives it a little bit more ….. sparkle.

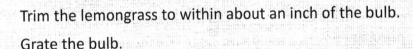

HARU GIMLET

For the infused gin....

- 1 x stick lemongrass
- 1.5 x tbsp grated fresh ginger
- 1 x tsp grated lime zest
- 375ml x Roku gin

Trim the lemongrass to within about an inch of the bulb.

Grate the bulb.

Add all the ingredients to a clean jar and leave, sealed, to infuse for 24 hours.

Fine strain the contents into a sterilised glass bottle and seal. Keep refrigerated.

For the cocktail....

1.5 x infused gin

0.5 x fresh lime juice

0.25 x elderflower cordial

0.15 x sugar syrup

Add ice and all the ingredients to a shaker. Shake vigorously until well chilled.

Strain into a chilled coupe glass.

During the time of Lockdown Saturday Cocktail 'Hour', friends have, occasionally, suggested various concoctions to me. This is one such cocktail.

I had never heard of it; nor was I familiar with this brand of Japanese gin.

Obviously, to serve it, it has to be planned a few days in advance. Our verdict was that it is well worth the planning and the faff.

Week 55 (Part 1)

PENICILLIN

- 2 x blended Scotch
- 0.8 x honey-ginger syrup
- 0.8 x lemon juice
- 0.25 x Islay single malt whisky

Add ice and the blended Scotch, lemon juice and syrup to a shaker.

Shake vigorously until well chilled.

Strain into a whiskey, or suitable, glass over ice cubes.

Gently top with the Islay single malt.

Garnish with candied ginger.

To make the honey-ginger syrup....

Peel and thinly slice 100g root ginger. Place in a saucepan with 1 cup of runny honey and 1 cup of water. Bring to the boil and simmer for 5 minutes. Cool and refrigerate in a sealed container for, at least, 12 hours. Finely strain and bottle before use.

The very distinct, peaty, flavour of the Islay whiskey, despite being a small quantity comes through. If this is not to your liking, a A MOCK SICILLIN (see next page) may be more palatable.

Week 55 (Sunday Addendum)

A MOCK SICILLIN

- 2 x blended Scotch
- 1 x honey-ginger syrup
- Soda water
- 1 x lemon juice
- 0.5 x ginger wine

Add ice and the blended Scotch, lemon juice, syrup and ginger wine to a shaker.

Shake vigorously until well chilled.

Strain into a highball glass over fresh ice and top with soda water.

Cathy was not a fan of the peaty flavour of the Penicillin. (To be honest, I am unlikely to choose it from a cocktail list.)

She replaced the Islay Malt with ginger wine and, whilst changing the flavour completely, a new, very acceptable, cocktail was born.

I christened it A Mock Sicillin.

Week 56

HUGO

- 1 x gin
- Prosecco
- Lime
- 0.5 x elderflower cordial
- Soda water
- Mint leaves

Half fill a wine glass with ice and pour in the gin and elderflower cordial.

Tuck in 3 or 4 mint leaves and squeeze, then drop in, a lime wedge.

Stir to mix.

Top up with prosecco and stir again.

Add a splash of soda water on top and drop in a couple of frozen blueberries.

Cathy, first, tasted a Hugo while on a business trip to Munich. Since then, she has mentioned it many times.

It is a very refreshing sunny summer drink and always available at our house.

03 May 2021 – My Second Vaccination

That's that then, my second vaccination dose is in my arm;
Like the first, I'm sure it will work like a charm
And keep me safe from serious infection
So that I can end, from the rest of the world, my current disconnection.

Yet, still some countries have many thousands falling ill.
The infections are still rising in India and Brazil
Whose ruling bodies seem to be oblivious to the fact
That their countryman's health is being ransacked.

The hope is that all the countries of the world will be inoculated
And, then, far away travel will become deregulated.
I will be happy to, always, take with me, documentation,
That proves I will not be an infectious danger to my destination.

But first, simple things like shopping and eating inside
A restaurant; things we used to take in our stride
Will be possible again, here, and it will be oh! so nice
But only after we've all been vaccinated twice.

We should all give thanks to the staff and volunteers
Who have put on hold their free time and, some, their own careers
To help our NHS make this country safe again with a couple of jabs
Of serum from, in my case, AstraZeneca's sterilised labs.

Week 57

LEMON DROP

For the glass rim....

Mix 1 tbsp of white castor sugar with the zest of half a lemon (grated or finely chopped).

- 2 x vodka
- 1 x triple sec
- 1 x lemon juice (freshly squeezed)

Add ice and the ingredients to a shaker and shake vigorously until well chilled.

Wet and shake the rim of a chilled martini glass and dip in the sugar mixture.

Strain the contents of the shaker into the glass.

The zesty sugar on the rim of the glass is essential for the overall flavour and feeling of the cocktail. Without it, the flavour is a little too zesty.

11 May 2021 – What's Been Missed The Most?

Wishing for the end of Lockdown, we've all had our own priorities,
Waiting for the required permission from the government's authorities.
Be it for visiting friends, going to the cinema or indoor dining
There have been many things, for which all of us have been pining.

What's been missed most, whilst the world has remained closed?
What do you look forward to doing, post lockdown, unopposed?
Or are you quite content with the way your life has changed?
And there is nothing you've missed from which you've been estranged.

I know, for some, it was the taste of that first pint in a pub
Especially for those with a social life whose local is the hub.
Happy to sit outside in the sun and, occasionally, the rain
But it didn't matter because their lives had begun again.

Or was it an early appointment at the hairdressing stylist?
As soon as possible, was a professional cut top of your to do list?
For many, shopping for clothes and, after so long, a wardrobe re-stock
With queues to enter Primark stretching all around the block.

For me, none of the above held much of a burning desire;
Except, for lunch at the Club, my enthusiasm couldn't have been higher.
To get to a hairdresser, I didn't think I needed to be quite so nippy
Happy, as I am, to have hair as long as during my days as a hippy.

Week 58

THE VACCINE

- 1 x vodka
- 1 x tequila
- 1 x Giffard Crème Pamplemousse Pink Grapefruit Liqueur
- 0.5 x Triple Sec
- 0.5 x lime juice (freshly squeezed)
- 2 x orange juice (freshly squeezed)

Add ice and all the ingredients to a shaker. Shake vigorously until well chilled.

Strain into a chilled coup glass.

Garnish with health and happiness.

My own invention to celebrate being doubly vaccinated.

Just like its namesake, that is administered using a syringe, this will make you feel happy about the future and have a kick that makes you know you've had something special.

Week 59

WOO WOO

- 2 x vodka
- 4 x cranberry juice
- 1 x peach schnapps
- A few drops of freshly squeezed lime juice

Add ice and all the ingredient to a shaker and shake vigorously until well chilled.

Squeeze and drop in a lime wedge to a cocktail jar, add ice and strain in the contents of the shaker.

Today, I had my first haircut since January 2020. A visit to the hairdresser was never a top priority and I was happy to have hair as long as it was in my 1970s hippy days. Cutting it now was a symbolic gesture that, for me, meant lockdown days are nearing their end and my life is returning to a new form of normality.

This is a very refreshing fruity cocktail. However, show it some respect because it can, very easily, creep up on you.

29 May 2021 – Trouble in Westminster

A number of milestones have been, recently, passed.
I've had a haircut - at long last
And, yesterday, for the first time this year
Indoor lunching in a safe and friendly atmosphere.

Although, "Lockdown Rules" still exist, they have been eased
Which makes everyone in England exceptionally pleased.
And, despite the "Indian Variant" causing a rise in infection
We all hope for no change to Boris's roadmap projection.

This week, in Westminster, however, the air turned red
When, in a joint parliamentary committee, ugly words were said
By Dominic Cummings; but he admitted he'd been, previously, lying
When, last summer, unusual eye tests he'd been applying.

He claimed that Boris was not, and never had been, a fit Prime Minister
Claims that, any sensible British voter must find extremely sinister
Because, as Boris's campaign manager in the leadership election race,
It is down to Mr Cummings that he was installed in Downing Street, in the first place.

But, of course, Boris claims that anything he says cannot be believed
And he is only making these claims because he is, clearly, aggrieved
At having been, as Senior Cabinet Adviser, summarily, fired.
Perhaps, then, you Blonde Haired Buffoon, he should never have been hired.

It's the weekend and the sun is shining so everyone has a smile
And thoughts of all these political liars are behind us for a while.
We'll be on the deck for tonight's Lockdown Saturday Cocktail time,
Which is coming very soon! so I'd better end, now, this little rhyme.

Week 60

RASPBERRY ROSÉ COOLER

- 1 x white rum
- 1 x raspberry lemonade
- fresh raspberries

- 4 x rosé
- 1 x dash orange bitters

Muddle three or four raspberries in the bottom of a mixing glass.

Add ice and the rum, rosé and orange bitters to the glass and stir until well chilled.

Double strain from the mixing glass into a wine glass then add the raspberry lemonade.

Garnish with a couple of frozen raspberries.

Another of my own recipes. This is a very refreshing long drink for a hot, sunny afternoon. The recipe shows a 1-4 ratio of rum to rosé, however, 1-5 would be just as acceptable.

Week 61

VESPER

- 3 x gin
- 1 x vodka
- 0.5 x Lillet Blanc

Add ice and all the ingredients to a mixing glass and stir until well chilled.

Strain into a chilled cocktail glass.

Squeeze a lemon twist to express the oils over the drink, rub the twist around the rim of the glass then drop it into the glass.

This martini is named after Vesper Lynd from the first James Bond novel, 'Casino Royale'. The recipe, in the 2006 movie, is described as 'Three measures of Gordon's; one of vodka; half a measure of Kina Lillet. Shake it over ice, and add a thin slice of lemon peel.'

This is my version and ideal for someone who can't decide between a gin martini and a vodka martini.

Week 62

THAI ME UP THAI ME DOWN

For the Thai basil infused sake....

Take 5 or 6 Thai basil leaves and squeeze gently. Add the leaves and about half a bottle of sake* to a jar. Seal and shake gently. Leave to infuse for 2 or 3 days.

For the kaffir lime leaf syrup....

Add about 10 leaves to a simple sugar syrup. Bottle and leave to infuse for a few hours.

For the cocktail....

- 2 x vodka
- 2 x Thai basil infused sake
- 0.75 x lime juice (freshly squeezed)
- 0.75 x kaffir lime leaf syrup
- 2 x dashes yuzu bitters
- soda water (optional)

Add ice and all the ingredients, except soda water, to a shaker.
Shake vigorously until well chilled.
Add ice to a medium highball glass.
Strain into the highball glass
and garnish with a sprig of mint.
Optionally, top with soda water.

* I used Akashi-Tai Ginjo Yuzushu. It is made by macerating yuzu in ginjo-grade sake. It has a crisp and fresh taste with zesty grapefruit and lime notes. It is ideal for this zesty citrus cocktail.

Week 63

FRENCH LADY

- 2 x gin
- 1 x Lillet Blanc
- 2 x grapefruit juice
- 1 x Teisseire Citron

Add ice and all the ingredients to a shaker.

Shake vigorously until well chilled.

Strain into a chilled martini glass and garnish with a grapefruit twist.

20 June 2021 – Freedom Day Delayed

So, tomorrow, June 21st was going to be "Freedom Day";
But, no surprise, last week, Boris announced there'd be a delay.
The, so-called, 'Delta' variant, running rampant, is the reason why
So the date of Freedom Day's gone back a month to the 19th of July.

In another month, will the situation be better or worse?
Will the variant have had enough time to reduce and disperse?
Or, come that day, will Boris announce another new dateline?
Frankly, your guess is as good as his, or mine.

However, undaunted, we soldier on with our stiff upper lips
Each coping, in our own way, with this current apocalypse.
And so, for the moment, we remain restricted, as we were before,
Except at weddings and funerals; the number of guests can be more.

Like everyone else, I'll wait, and my breath I'll bate
In the hope that our leader will not, again, procrastinate
And allow us to return to a new form of normal lifestyle,
All doubly vaccinated against the infection that is so hostile.

Life will, probably, never be the same as it was, pre-March last year
There will, forever, be new rules and regulations to which we'll have to adhere.
But that will be a small price to pay if, our global freedom they permit
And I for one, to them all, will happily, submit.

Week 64 (Cathy's Birthday)

BIRTHDAY SPARKLER

- 2 x gin
- 1 x Lillet Blanc
- 2 x grapefruit juice
- 1 x Teisseire Lemon

Add all the ingredients to a shaker.

Shake until mixed.

Strain into clean bottles. Make as many as required and chill until the party.

To serve, half fill a glass with 'The Lady' and top with Prosecco.

Basically, a French Lady + Bubbles.

This is an excellent party cocktail (but not for those on statins).

The French Lady portion should be mixed a day or two earlier and chilled.

At the party, simply mix with chilled Prosecco for a fun, sunny cocktail, whatever the weather.

28 June 2021 - Postface

As I write this, June 26th has now come and, then, gone
But the worldwide Covid pandemic still drags on.
If I were to continue mixing cocktails until its eradication
I'd spend the rest of my life concocting a new weekly libation.

It was fitting, in the sun, with a few friends invited
To mix and pass round 'Birthday Sparklers', which delighted
Every one of our guests for all of the afternoon
And well after the rising of the moon.

The past year and a half has been a struggle for all the world's populace;
To develop a life-saving vaccine, so many scientists joined in the race.
I did what I could to help a few get through these dreadful times
By mixing drinks in glasses and writing some silly little rhymes.

THE RHYMES

About the Author

George Forsyth was born in Glasgow in 1952 but was brought up and educated in Aberdeen. After school, he moved to Edinburgh and completed a diploma in Computer Studies. In 1977, he moved to London and worked with the computerisation of advertising for a number of commercial television companies until his retirement in May 2017. Since his retirement and before the Covid pandemic of 2020, he spent a lot of time travelling the world visiting friends and seeing new places. His only previous published work is a letter in the British Airways in-flight magazine, "High Life". He his married to his second wife, Cathy, and lives in West Sussex.

Lightning Source UK Ltd.
Milton Keynes UK
UKHW051148131121
393903UK00006B/58